BE *Still,* RECEIVE

Grace AND *Peace*

PEARL

WESTBOW
. PRESS®
A DIVISION OF THOMAS NELSON
& ZONDERVAN

WestBow Press books may be ordered through booksellers or by contacting:

WestBow Press
A Division of Thomas Nelson & Zondervan
1663 Liberty Drive
Bloomington, IN 47403
www.westbowpress.com
1 (866) 928-1240

ISBN: 978-1-5127-0260-6 (sc)
ISBN: 978-1-5127-0259-0 (e)

Library of Congress Control Number: 2015911475

Print information available on the last page.

WestBow Press rev. date: 07/16/2015

This devotion was written to be used with your bible every day. To be with the Lord you must be in the word, and the word is the bible.

To write the scripture and to explain what that scripture means to you at this season in your life allows you to interact with God. To go to him daily is like going to, and seeing a good friend or the desire to spend time with that friend.

JANUARY 1

Jesus loves me! This I know,
For the Bible tells me so.
Little ones to Him belong;
They are weak, but He is strong.

Chorus:
Yes, Jesus loves me!
Yes, Jesus loves me!
Yes, Jesus loves me!
The Bible tells me so.

Jesus loves me! This I know,
As He loved so long ago,
Taking children on His knee,
Saying "Let them come to Me."

Chorus:
Yes, Jesus loves me!
Yes, Jesus loves me!
Yes, Jesus loves me!
The Bible tells me so.

Jesus loves me when I'm good,
When I do the things I should,
Jesus loves me when I'm bad,
Though it makes Him very sad.

Chorus:
Yes, Jesus loves me!
Yes, Jesus loves me!
Yes, Jesus loves me!
The Bible tells me so.

Jesus loves me still today,
Walking with me on my way,
Wanting as a friend to give
Light and love to all who live.

Chorus:
Yes, Jesus loves me!
Yes, Jesus loves me!
Yes, Jesus loves me!
The Bible tells me so.

Jesus loves me! He who died
Heaven's gate to open wide;
He will wash away my sin,
Let His little child come in.

Chorus:
Yes, Jesus loves me!
Yes, Jesus loves me!
Yes, Jesus loves me!
The Bible tells me so.

Jesus loves me! Loves me still
Tho' I'm very weak and ill;
That I might from sin be free
Bled and died upon the tree.

Chorus:
Yes, Jesus loves me!
Yes, Jesus loves me!
Yes, Jesus loves me!
The Bible tells me so.

Jesus loves me! He will stay
Close beside me all the way;
Thou hast bled and died for me,
I will henceforth live for Thee.

Chorus:
Yes, Jesus loves me!
Yes, Jesus loves me!
Yes, Jesus loves me!
The Bible tells me so.

Does this bring back memories, how do
you feel about Jesus loves you?

JANUARY 2

When God takes one of His children and uses them in a mighty way, He chooses the one who is available. He knows the weaknesses and strengths, the talents and the gifts. He also knows the breaking points.

JANUARY 3

There is nothing I can do to make God love me more.

There is nothing I can do to make God love me less.

Grace…

My thoughts are not your thoughts,
neither are your ways my way,
declares the LORD.
As the heavens are higher than the earth,
so are my ways higher than your ways
and my thoughts than your thoughts.

JANUARY 4

Forgiveness is an unnatural act.

It is this act that sets a Christian apart from others.

As we pray for our enemies, we are doing for
them what they cannot do for themselves.

The gospel of grace begins and ends with forgiveness.
Forgiveness is and the act of faith.

By releasing my own right of revenge, I
leave all fairness in God's hands.

"It is mine to avenge; I will repay" says the LORD.

I leave in God's hands the scales that
must balance justice and mercy.

Forgiveness is not easy, and definitely not satisfying. Satan uses
the venom of injustice to keep the wound open and cause pain.
We approach God again and again, giving to him morsels
of what we thought we had committed to him many times
before. Only by living in the well of God's grace will we find
the strength to respond in grace with grace, toward others.

JANUARY 5

I believe life is more than survival

I believe the heart is more than a muscle

I believe in hope and freedom

I believe we can know right from wrong

I believe my life can make a difference

I believe the message of the cross

What do you believe?

JANUARY 6

Forgiveness offers a way out. It does not settle all questions of blame and fairness, often it out right evades those questions, but it does allow a relationship to start over, to begin anew.

Our capacity to think makes us different from all other animals. Our capacity to repent, and forgive makes us different also. Innocent with no hint of wrong, or guilty wholly to blame, each will bear the wound until they find a way to release it, forgiveness... no blame admitted or denied, or no fingers pointed, each allowed to move on, even set pride aside. Satan does not like that.

What Satan likes is to imprison within the walls of pride; imprison in the past and locks all potential for the future or change.

When we genuinely forgive, who is the prisoner we release?

How can we not forgive each other after all God has forgiven us?

JANUARY 7

Was the elephant in the room not discussed because it would offend the person with the money? Was the organization so in need of money, it didn't matter where it came from? The good deed of the money over rides the hell it came from...

To the banquet Jesus welcomed tax collectors and murders. He came for the sick and not the well, for the unrighteous and not the righteous. To those who betrayed him, including the disciples, who forsook him at his time of greatest need, he responded like a lovesick father.

Did the Pastor request a lay speaker for the lesson, so not to reveal the true feeling on the subject to the congregation?

We looked away, walked blocks out of our way, not to greet or face a person and their situation.

Society encourages ignoring a person or situation;

It won't hurt if I don't look at or acknowledge it
By not dealing with it, it will go away.
Don't tell the truth or hurt some ones
feelings and it will also go away.
If I acknowledge it, it means I agree with it.

JANUARY 8

In the Old Testament stories the scandal of grace ripples under
the surface until finally, in Jesus' parables, grace erupts in
to a dramatic realization, reshaping the moral landscape.

Was he giving us a parable of grace? Grace cannot be
calculated as money, like wages? Grace is a gift from God, not
something we sweat and feel we earn. A point Jesus made
clear. The employer stated, "I am not being unfair to you.
Didn't you agree to work for that amount of money? Take your
pay and go. If I want to give the man who was hired last the
same I give you; don't I have the right to do what I want with
my own money? Are you envious because I am generous?

No one was cheated. Discontent rose from the human's
conception of fairness, not grace. Workers could not accept that
the employer had the right to do what he wanted with his money.

God dispenses gifts, not wages. If paid on the
basis of fairness, we would all end up in hell.

JANUARY 9

Living in this modern time when the world is torn by terrorism; when leaders of countries and nations cannot move without protection; mutiny stalks the earth; we wonder how we could face the suffering. Starvation is surrounded by ease and freedom; slavery is unthinkable but common in the black market. We read, hear, and see those who are examples of unbelievable courage, do you ask, "Could I survive such circumstances, and keep my sanity?" (1)

Would you be surprised to find out this was written in 1959 by the Queen of Denmark?

Then repeated in 1983 by Corrie ten Boom...

How little has our world changed?

JANUARY 10   PSALM 32:8-9

Write the verse(s) from your bible here. Then
write how you think it touches you.

JANUARY 11 PSALM 31:23-24

Write the verse(s) from your bible here. Then
write how you think it touches you.

JANUARY 12   DUET 18:9-12

Write the verse(s) from your bible here. Then
write how you think it touches you.

JANUARY 13

The fear of demons comes from demons
themselves; Jesus is Victor.
Luke 9:1 & Luke 10:17 How will you deal with fear?

JANUARY 14   1JOHN 1:5-10

Write the verse(s) from your bible here. Then
write how you think it touches you.

JANUARY 15   ROMANS 8:26-27

Write the verse(s) from your bible here. Then
write how you think it touches you.

The Believer's Triumph

What then are we to say about these things?
If God is for us, who is against us?
He did not even spare His own Son, but offered Him up
for us all; how will He not also with Him grant us everything?
Who can bring an accusation against God's elect?
God is the One who justifies.
Who is the one who condemns?
Christ Jesus is the One who died, but even more, has been raised;
He also is at the right hand of God and intercedes for us.
Who can separate us from the love of Christ?
Can affliction or anguish or persecution or famine
or nakedness or danger or sword?
As it is written:
Because of You we are being put to death all day long;
we are counted as sheep to be slaughtered.
No, in all these things we are more than victorious
through Him who loved us.
For I am persuaded that neither death nor life, nor
angels nor rulers, nor things present, nor things to come,
nor powers, nor height, nor depth, nor any other
created thing will have the power to separate us from
the love of God that is in Christ Jesus our Lord!

JANUARY 17 PSALM 91

The Protection of the Most High

The one who lives under the protection of the Most High dwells
in the shadow of the Almighty
I will say to the LORD,
"My refuge and my fortress, my God, in whom I trust."
He Himself will deliver you from the hunter's net,
from the destructive plague.
He will cover you with His feathers;
you will take refuge under His wings.
His faithfulness will be a protective shield.
You will not fear the terror of the night,
the arrow that flies by day,
the plague that stalks in darkness,
or the pestilence that ravages at noon.
Though a thousand fall at your side
and ten thousand at your right hand,
the pestilence will not reach you.
You will only see it with your eyes
and witness the punishment of the wicked.
Because you have made the LORD—my refuge,
the Most High—your dwelling place,
no harm will come to you;
no plague will come near your tent.
For He will give His angels orders concerning you,
to protect you in all your ways.
They will support you with their hands
so that you will not strike your foot against a stone.

You will tread on the lion and the cobra;
you will trample the young lion and the serpent.
Because he is lovingly devoted to Me, I will deliver him;
I will exalt him because he knows My name.
When he calls out to Me, I will answer him;
I will be with him in trouble.
I will rescue him and give him honor.
I will satisfy him with a long life and show him My salvation.

JANUARY 18

Limited physical circumstance as a human, life
is made in the image of God; it is precious and
worth living to the fullest of His blessings.
Matthew 22:37-40

Jesus said to him, "Love the Lord your God with all your heart,
with all your soul, and with all your mind. This is the greatest and
most important commandment. The second is like it: Love your
neighbor as yourself. All the Law and the Prophets depend on
these two commandments."

JANUARY 19 PSALM 23

Read it not as you would hear it at a funeral, but
as if Jesus is talking to you to follow him.
Write the verse(s) from your bible here. Then
write how you think it touches you.

JANUARY 20

I _____

(Print your name)

belong to the one true living

God. I am a holy child of God

I have the Holy Spirit of the

one living God in my heart.

The LORD of heaven &

earth has declared me

"His Holy Vessel". I commit to believing His word in scripture

"I am holy". Encourage & empower me daily with people, your

Holy Spirit & the Holy scriptures, to humbly treat myself as holy.

Allow the schemes of the enemy to be thwarted because I have

your protection.

You are my God.

Your word is truth.

This day father

I chose to believe

You. In the name

of your son Jesus Christ,

Amen

JANUARY 21   PSALM 119:33-39

Write the verse(s) from your bible here. Then
write how you think it touches you.

Do not be conformed to this age, but be transformed
by the renewing of your mind, so that you may discern
what is the good, pleasing, and perfect will of God.

Many Gifts but One Body

For by the grace given to me, I tell everyone among you not
to think of yourself more highly than you should. Instead,
think sensibly, as God has distributed a measure of faith to
each one. Now as we have many parts in one body, and all
the parts do not have the same function, in the same way
we who are many are one body in Christ and individually
members of one another. According to the grace given to
us, we have different gifts: If prophecy, use it according to
the standard of faith; if service, in service; if teaching,
in teaching; if exhorting, in exhortation; giving, with generosity;
leading, with diligence; showing mercy, with cheerfulness.

Christian Ethics

Love must be without hypocrisy. Detest evil; cling to what is good. Show family affection to one another with brotherly love. Outdo one another in showing honor. Do not lack diligence; be fervent in spirit; serve the Lord. Rejoice in hope; be patient in affliction; be persistent in prayer. Share with the saints in their needs; pursue hospitality. Bless those who persecute you; bless and do not curse. Rejoice with those who rejoice; weep with those who weep. Be in agreement with one another. Do not be proud; instead, associate with the humble. Do not be wise in your own estimation. Do not repay anyone evil for evil. Try to do what is honorable in everyone's eyes. If possible, on your part, live at peace with everyone. Friends, do not avenge yourselves; instead, leave room for His wrath. For it is written: **Vengeance belongs to Me; I will repay,** says the Lord. But **If your enemy is hungry, feed him. If he is thirsty, give him something to drink. For in so doing you will be heaping fiery coals on his head.** Do not be conquered by evil, but conquer evil with good.

JANUARY 24   EPHESIANS 2:1-10

From Death to Life

Write the verse(s) from your bible here. Then
write how you think it touches you.

JANUARY 25   GALATIANS 2:16

Write the verse(s) from your bible here. Then
write how you think it touches you.

JANUARY 26   GALATIANS 3:19-26

The Purpose of the Law

Write the verse(s) from your bible here. Then
write how you think it touches you.

JANUARY 27   ROMANS 8:12-17

The Holy Spirit's Ministries

Write the verse(s) from your bible here. Then
write how you think it touches you.

JANUARY 28 ROMANS 15:8-17

Christ like Love

Write the verse(s) from your bible here. Then
write how you think it touches you.

JANUARY 29   ROMANS 10:14-18

Write the verse(s) from your bible here. Then
write how you think it touches you.

JANUARY 30   ROMANS 1:16-17

The Righteous Will Live by Faith

Write the verse(s) from your bible here. Then
write how you think it touches you.

JANUARY 31

Grace does not depend on what we have done
for God, but what God has done for us.

Reflection: Most precious God. You have given me all that
I have, and yet I only ask for more. Please know I love
you. I appreciate all you do and give me. Do not think for a
minute that I do not know where my material and spiritual
wealth come from. Praise you LORD for you grace and your
mercy. Allow me to share it with those you see fit. Allow
me to discern who that is and how to accomplish this.

In the name of your son, Jesus Christ, Amen.

FEBRUARY 1   REV: 9-24

"Come, I will show you the bride, the wife of the Lamb"

Write the verse(s) from your bible here. Then
write how you think it touches you.

_____

FEBRUARY 2   1 PETER 4:21-22

Write the verse(s) from your bible here. Then
write how you think it touches you.

FEBRUARY 3   EPH 5:15

Compliance, surrender, obey God

How are you going to accomplish this completely?

FEBRUARY 4   MATTHEW 18:10

The Parable of the Lost Sheep

Write the verse(s) from your bible here. Then
write how you think it touches you.

FEBRUARY 5   1 TIMOTHY 6:17-19

Instructions to the Rich

Write the verse(s) from your bible here. Then
write how you think it touches you.

FEBRUARY 6 JAMES 7:13-18

Effective Prayer

Write the verse(s) from your bible here. Then
write how you think it touches you.

FEBRUARY 7   ISAIAH 43:25

Pleasure is good, wanting more, an abundance of it
is Satan; never enough, want more, more, more....
Leading each day, little by little, to disobedience.

What are the seven deadly sins given in the bible?

Write the verse(s) from your bible here. Then
write how you think it touches you.

_____

FEBRUARY 8 MATTHEW 11:28-30

Write the verse(s) from your bible here. Then
write how you think it touches you.

FEBRUARY 9   DUET 32:7

God heals it

Write the verse(s) from your bible here. Then
write how you think it touches you.

FEBRUARY 10   EPH 1:4-6

God's Rich Blessings

Write the verse(s) from your bible here. Then
write how you think it touches you.

FEBRUARY 11　1 JOHN 4:7-16

Knowing God through Love

Write the verse(s) from your bible here. Then
write how you think it touches you.

FEBRUARY 12   JOHN 16:32-33

Jesus said to them...

Write the verse(s) from your bible here. Then
write how you think it touches you.

FEBRUARY 13   1 COR 2:9

But as it is written:

Write the verse(s) from your bible here. Then write how you think it touches you.

FEBRUARY 14   LAM 3:28

God meets us in our humanity

FEBRUARY 15   ROMANS 8:12-17

The Holy Spirit's Ministries

Write the verse(s) from your bible here. Then write how you think it touches you.

FEBRUARY 16   ROMANS 8:26-27

In the same way the Spirit also joins to help in our weakness...

Write the verse(s) from your bible here. Then
write how you think it touches you.

FEBRUARY 17   ROMANS 8:31-39

The Believer's Triumph

Write the verse(s) from your bible here. Then
write how you think it touches you.

FEBRUARY 18   LUKE 8:1-3

Many Women Support Christ's Work

Write the verse(s) from your bible here. Then
write how you think it touches you.

FEBRUARY 19   LUKE 8:40-56

A Girl Restored and a Woman Healed

Write the verse(s) from your bible here. Then
write how you think it touches you.

How to Pray

"Whenever you pray, you must not be like the hypocrites, because they love to pray standing in the synagogues and on the street corners to be seen by people. I assure you: They've got their reward! But when you pray, go into your private room, shut your door, and pray to your Father who is in secret. And your Father who sees in secret will reward you. When you pray, don't babble like the idolaters, since they imagine they'll be heard for their many words. Don't be like them, because your Father knows the things you need before you ask Him.

FEBRUARY 21   MATTHEW 6:19-24

God and Possessions

Write the verse(s) from your bible here. Then
write how you think it touches you.

FEBRUARY 22   MATTHEW 12:38-42

Then some of the scribes and Pharisees
said to Him, "Teacher, we want to see a sign
from You." But He answered them,

Write the verse(s) from your bible here. Then
write how you think it touches you.

FEBRUARY 23   LUKE 10:38-42

Martha and Mary

Write the verse(s) from your bible here. Then
write how you think it touches you.

FEBRUARY 24   LUKE 13:10-17

Healing a Daughter of Abraham

Write the verse(s) from your bible here. Then
write how you think it touches you.

FEBRUARY 25   LUKE 14:10-17

Healing a Daughter of Abraham

Write the verse(s) from your bible here. Then
write how you think it touches you.

———————————————————

FEBRUARY 26   LUKE 15:10-17

Healing a Daughter of Abraham

Write the verse(s) from your bible here. Then
write how you think it touches you.

FEBRUARY 27   LUKE 18:1-8

The Parable of the Persistent Widow

Write the verse(s) from your bible here. Then
write how you think it touches you.

FEBRUARY 28   LUKE 20:9-19

The Parable of the Vineyard Owner

Write the verse(s) from your bible here. Then
write how you think it touches you.

FEBRUARY 29   LUKE 21:1-4

The Widow's Gift

Write the verse(s) from your bible here. Then
write how you think it touches you.

MARCH 1   MATTHEW 12:43-45

An Unclean Spirit's Return

Write the verse(s) from your bible here. Then
write how you think it touches you.

MARCH 2 MATTHEW 15:10-20

Defilement Is from Within

Write the verse(s) from your bible here. Then
write how you think it touches you.

MARCH 3   MATTHEW 15:21-28

A Gentile Mother's Faith

Write the verse(s) from your bible here. Then
write how you think it touches you.

MARCH 4   MATTHEW 19:1-12

The Question of Divorce

Write the verse(s) from your bible here. Then
write how you think it touches you.

MARCH 5   MATTHEW 20:1-16

The Parable of the Vineyard Workers

Write the verse(s) from your bible here. Then
write how you think it touches you.

MARCH 6   MATTHEW 24:36-44

No One Knows the Day or Hour

Write the verse(s) from your bible here. Then
write how you think it touches you.

MARCH 7   MATTHEW 25:1-13

The Parable of the 10 Virgins

Write the verse(s) from your bible here. Then
write how you think it touches you.

_____

MARCH 8   JOHN 15:1-8

The Vine and the Branches

Write the verse(s) from your bible here. Then
write how you think it touches you.

MARCH 9 JOHN 16:25-33

Jesus the Victor

Write the verse(s) from your bible here. Then
write how you think it touches you.

MARCH 10   JOHN 20:11-18

Mary Magdalene Sees the Risen Lord

Write the verse(s) from your bible here. Then
write how you think it touches you.

MARCH 11   JOHN 20:30-31

The Purpose of This Gospel

Write the verse(s) from your bible here. Then
write how you think it touches you.

MARCH 12   PROVERBS 1:1-7

The Purpose of Proverbs

Write the verse(s) from your bible here. Then
write how you think it touches you.

MARCH 13   PROVERBS 2:1-22

Wisdom's Worth

Write the verse(s) from your bible here. Then
write how you think it touches you.

_____

MARCH 14   PROVERBS 3:13-26

Wisdom Brings Happiness

Write the verse(s) from your bible here. Then write how you think it touches you.

MARCH 15   PROVERBS 3:27-35

Treat Others Fairly

Write the verse(s) from your bible here. Then
write how you think it touches you.

MARCH 16   PROVERBS 4:20-27

Write the verse(s) from your bible here. Then
write how you think it touches you.

MARCH 17   PROVERBS 5:15-23

Enjoy Marriage

Write the verse(s) from your bible here. Then
write how you think it touches you.

MARCH 18   PROVERBS 6:16-19

Six things the LORD hates; in fact, seven are detestable to Him:

Write the verse(s) from your bible here. Then
write how you think it touches you.

===

MARCH 19   PROVERBS 6:20-35

Warning against Adultery

Write the verse(s) from your bible here. Then
write how you think it touches you.

MARCH 20   PROVERBS 8:1-36

Wisdom's Appeal

Write the verse(s) from your bible here. Then
write how you think it touches you.

MARCH 21   PROVERBS 11:24-25

Write the verse(s) from your bible here. Then
write how you think it touches you.

MARCH 26   PROVERBS 12:4-6

Write the verse(s) from your bible here. Then
write how you think it touches you.

MARCH 27   PROVERBS 14:1, 10, 17, 2-31

Write the verse(s) from your bible here. Then
write how you think it touches you.

MARCH 28   COLOSSIANS 2:16-19

Write the verse(s) from your bible here. Then
write how you think it touches you.

MARCH 29   EPHESIANS 2:10

For we are His creation—

Write the verse(s) from your bible here. Then
write how you think it touches you.

MARCH 30   PSALM 75:6-7

Write the verse(s) from your bible here. Then
write how you think it touches you.

MARCH 31   PSALM 22

From Suffering to Praise

Write the verse(s) from your bible here. Then
write how you think it touches you.

APRIL 1   MICAH 7:18-20

Write the verse(s) from your bible here. Then
write how you think it touches you.

APRIL 2   2 CORINTHIANS 10:3-6

For although we are walking in the flesh...

Write the verse(s) from your bible here. Then
write how you think it touches you.

What do you think... The three pillars of Christian foundation: Faith, Grace, Scripture

I needed more information on these terms. What do each of the words mean; the definition of each? And, if I were to need synonyms for each for each of them, to better explain each, what would I use?

Faith: An allegiance; belief and trust in God; confidence; system of religious beliefs.

Synonyms: belief, credence, credit, trust, confidence, dependence, hope, reliance, stock, religion, creed, cult, persuasion, sect, church, communion, connection, denomination, persuasion

Grace: unmerited divine assistance; A short prayer after a meal; respite
Ease of movement or bearing; Honor; Adorn

Synonyms: benediction, blessing, thanks, thanksgiving, mercy, charity, clemency, lenity, elegance, dignity.

Scripture: Bible, sacred writings of a religion
Synonyms: Bible, Book, Holy writ, sacred writ

I have faith by believing and trusting in God the Father, the Son, and the Holy Spirit

I am given Grace only because I believe In Christ, the son of God, who died on the cross for my sins.

I study the Christian Holy Bible as the word of God, breathed by God, to share with those who do not know his word yet.

APRIL 4   HEBREWS 11:1-22

—m—

Now faith is the reality of what is hoped
for, the proof of what is not seen.

Write the verse(s) from your bible here. Then
write how you think it touches you.

APRIL 5

Just Push

A man was sleeping one night in his cabin when suddenly his room filled with light, and God appeared. The Lord told the man he had work for him to do, and showed him a large rock in front of his cabin. The Lord explained that the man was to push against the rock with all his might...

So, this the man did, day after day. For many years he toiled from sunup to sundown, his shoulders set squarely against the cold, massive surface of the unmoving rock, pushing with all his might!

Each night the man returned to his cabin sore and worn out, Feeling that his whole day had been spent in vain. Since the man was showing discouragement, the Adversary (Satan) decided to enter the picture by placing thoughts into the weary mind: (He will do it every time)!

You have been pushing against that rock for a long time and it hasn't moved.' Thus, he gave the man the impression that the task was impossible and that he was a failure. These thoughts discouraged and disheartened the man.

Satan said, 'Why kill yourself over this? Just put in your time, giving just the minimum effort; and that will be good enough.'

That's what the weary man planned to do, but decided to make it a matter of Prayer and to take his troubled thoughts to The Lord.

'Lord,' he said, 'I have labored long and hard in Your Service, putting all my strength to do that which you have asked. Yet, after all this time, I have not even budged that rock by half a millimeter. What is wrong? Why am I failing?'

The Lord responded compassionately, "My friend, when I asked you to serve Me and you accepted, I told you that your task was to push against the rock with all of your strength, which you have done.

Never once did I mention to you that I expected you to move it.

Your task was to push. And now you come to Me with your strength spent, thinking that you have failed.

But, is that really so? Look at yourself. Your arms are strong and muscled, your back shiny and brown; your hands are callused from constant pressure, your legs have become massive and hard.

Through opposition you have grown much, and your abilities now surpass that which you used to have. True, you haven't moved the rock. But your calling was to be Obedient and to push and to exercise your Faith and trust in My wisdom. That you have done. Now I, my friend, will move the rock."

At times, when we hear a word from God, we tend to use our own intellect to decipher what He wants, when actually what God wants is just simple obedience and faith in Him.

By all means, exercise the Faith that moves mountains, but know that it is still God Who moves The Mountains.

When everything seems to go wrong.....................Just P.U.S.H.

When the job gets you down...............................Just P.U.S.H.

When people don't do as you think they should......Just P.U.S.H.

When your money is 'gone' and the bills are due......Just P.U.S.H.

When people just don't understand you.................Just P.U.S.H.

P = Pray

U = Until

S = Something

H = Happens

Write the verse(s)(s) from your bible here. Then
write how you think it touches you.

APRIL 7   PROVERBS 21:

Write the verse(s)(s) from your bible here. Then
write how you think it touches you.

APRIL 8   PROVERBS 23:4-5

Write the verse(s)(s) from your bible here. Then
write how you think it touches you.

APRIL 9   PROVERBS 23:19-23

Listen, my son, and be wise; keep your mind on the right course.

Write the verse(s)(s) from your bible here. Then
write how you think it touches you.

_____

APRIL 10 COLLISIONS 3:5-11

Write the verse(s) from your bible here. Then
write how you think it touches you.

APRIL 11   2 CORINTHIANS 5:17-21

Write the verse(s) from your bible here. Then
write how you think it touches you.

APRIL 12   1 PETER 3:13-17

Undeserved Suffering

Write the verse(s) from your bible here. Then
write how you think it touches you.

APRIL 13   ISAIAH 1:17-18

Write the verse(s) from your bible here. Then
write how you think it touches you.

APRIL 14   ISAIAH 45:17-18

Write the verse(s) from your bible here. Then
write how you think it touches you.

APRIL 15   JOB 38:1-7

The LORD Speaks

Write the verse(s) from your bible here. Then write how you think it touches you.

Write the verse(s) from your bible here. Then
write how you think it touches you.

APRIL 17   2 PETER 1:19-20

Write the verse(s) from your bible here. Then
write how you think it touches you.

APRIL 18   ROMANS 1:16

The Righteous Will Live by Faith

Write the verse(s) from your bible here. Then
write how you think it touches you.

APRIL 19 JEREMIAH 29:11-14

Write the verse(s) from your bible here. Then
write how you think it touches you.

APRIL 20   1 CORINTHIANS 13:4-8

Write the verse(s) from your bible here. Then
write how you think it touches you.

APRIL 21

Who is my enemy?
Who is killing our children?
Who is polluting our culture?
Who is threatening our morals?
Any enemy of God is an enemy of mine…

APRIL 22

Walk and talk in the manner of love:
Observe the rules of courtesy with everyone.
Love is giving until it hurts, & asking God to give more...

APRIL 23

You must empty yourself of hatred & anger. Empty all of your heart
and all your mind, allow God to fully enter in, allow Him to take
your pain and release His love. Hand it over to God, and leave it in
God's hands. How long has it taken for your to leave it with Him?

APRIL 24   LUKE 21:1-4

The Widow's Gift

Write the verse(s) from your bible here. Then
write how you think it touches you.

APRIL 25   LUKE 21:7-20

Signs of the End of the Age

Write the verse(s) from your bible here. Then
write how you think it touches you.

I prayed to the LORD my God and confessed:

Write the verse(s) from your bible here. Then
write how you think it touches you.

APRIL 27   EXODUS 28:15-21

The Breast piece

Write the verse(s) from your bible here. Then
write how you think it touches you.

The Bible tells us that not only was Egypt affected but all the surrounding countries were coming to Egypt to buy grain from Joseph. Because one man was willing to obey God, millions of people made it through seven years of famine. Can one person make a difference? The book of Geneses tells us how...

APRIL 29   MARK 7:1-23

Write the verse(s) from your bible here. Then
write how you think it touches you.

APRIL 30   MARK 7:24-30

A Gentile Mother's Faith

Write the verse(s) from your bible here. Then
write how you think it touches you.

MAY 1   EPHESIANS 5:15-21

Consistency in the Christian Life

Write the verse(s) from your bible here. Then
write how you think it touches you.

MAY 2   EPHESIANS 5:22-33

Wives and Husbands

Write the verse(s) from your bible here. Then
write how you think it touches you.

MAY 3   GALATIANS 3:10-18

Law and Promise

Write the verse(s) from your bible here. Then
write how you think it touches you.

MAY 4   GALATIANS 3:19-26

The Purpose of the Law

Write the verse(s) from your bible here. Then
write how you think it touches you.

MAY 5   2 CORINTHIANS 9:1-9

Motivations for Giving

Write the verse(s) from your bible here. Then
write how you think it touches you.

MAY 6   2 CORINTHIANS 13:11-13

Write the verse(s) from your bible here. Then
write how you think it touches you.

MAY 7 1 CORINTHIANS 13

—⫘—

Love: The Superior Way

Write the verse(s) from your bible here. Then
write how you think it touches you.

MAY 8   1 CORINTHIANS 2:6-9

Spiritual Wisdom

Write the verse(s) from your bible here. Then
write how you think it touches you.

MAY 9 1 CORINTHIANS 2:10-16

Write the verse(s) from your bible here. Then
write how you think it touches you.

MAY 10   1 CORINTHIANS 4:1-5

The Faithful Manager

Write the verse(s) from your bible here. Then
write how you think it touches you.

MAY 11 1 CORINTHIANS 5:1-8

Immoral Church Members

Write the verse(s) from your bible here. Then
write how you think it touches you.

MAY 12   1 CORINTHIANS 5:9-13

Church Discipline

Write the verse(s) from your bible here. Then
write how you think it touches you.

MAY 13   1 CORINTHIANS 6:13-17

Write the verse(s) from your bible here. Then
write how you think it touches you.

MAY 14   1 CORINTHIANS 7:1-7

Principles of Marriage

Write the verse(s) from your bible here. Then
write how you think it touches you.

MAY 15   1 CORINTHIANS 7:10-16

Advice to Married People

Write the verse(s) from your bible here. Then
write how you think it touches you.

MAY 16   1 CORINTHIANS 7:17-24

Various Situations of Life

Write the verse(s) from your bible here. Then
write how you think it touches you.

MAY 17   1 CORINTHIANS 10:14-22

Warning against Idolatry

Write the verse(s) from your bible here. Then
write how you think it touches you.

MAY 18   1CORINTHIANS 12:12-20

Write the verse(s) from your bible here. Then
write how you think it touches you.

MAY 19   ROMANS 8:3-6

Write the verse(s) from your bible here. Then
write how you think it touches you.

MAY 20   COLOSSIANS 3:5-11

Write the verse(s) from your bible here. Then
write how you think it touches you.

MAY 21   HEBREWS 3:7-11

Warning against Unbelief

Write the verse(s) from your bible here. Then
write how you think it touches you.

MAY 22   1 TIMOTHY 4:1-5

Write the verse(s) from your bible here. Then
write how you think it touches you.

MAY 23   HEBREWS 6:1-3

Write the verse(s) from your bible here. Then
write how you think it touches you.

MAY 24   HEBREWS 9:12-15

Write the verse(s) from your bible here. Then
write how you think it touches you.

MAY 25   HEBREWS 10:26-31

Write the verse(s) from your bible here. Then
write how you think it touches you.

The Holy Spirit Promised

Write the verse(s) from your bible here. Then write how you think it touches you.

MAY 27   JOHN 6:60-71

Many Disciples Desert Jesus

Write the verse(s) from your bible here. Then
write how you think it touches you.

MAY 29   ACTS 2:1-13

Pentecost

Write the verse(s) from your bible here. Then
write how you think it touches you.

MAY 30 ACTS 1:12-14

United in Prayer

Write the verse(s) from your bible here. Then
write how you think it touches you.

MAY 31   ACTS 2:32-36

Write the verse(s) from your bible here. Then
write how you think it touches you.

JUNE 1   ROMANS 8:12-17

The Holy Spirit's Ministries

Write the verse(s) from your bible here. Then
write how you think it touches you.

JUNE 2

Can you describe Christ in one or two words to someone? What are the names you come up with? Let's start with King of Kings, Lord of Lords... how many can you come up with?

JUNE 3   COLOSSIANS 1:9-14

Prayer for Spiritual Growth

Write the verse(s) from your bible here. Then
write how you think it touches you.

JUNE 4 2 CORINTHIANS 1:3-7

Write the verse(s) from your bible here. Then
write how you think it touches you.

JUNE 5   2 CORINTHIANS 1:8-11

Write the verse(s) from your bible here. Then
write how you think it touches you.

JUNE 6   2 CORINTHIANS 1:12-14

Write the verse(s) from your bible here. Then
write how you think it touches you.

JUNE 7   GALATIANS 4:1-7

Write the verse(s) from your bible here. Then
write how you think it touches you.

JUNE 8   ROMANS 8:18-25

Write the verse(s) from your bible here. Then
write how you think it touches you.

JUNE 9   ROMANS 8:26-27

Write the verse(s) from your bible here. Then
write how you think it touches you.

JUNE 10　ROMANS 8:28-30

Write the verse(s) from your bible here. Then
write how you think it touches you.

JUNE 11   ROMANS 8:31-35

Write the verse(s) from your bible here. Then
write how you think it touches you.

JUNE 12   ROMANS 8:38-39

Write the verse(s) from your bible here. Then
write how you think it touches you.

JUNE 13   JOHN 15:26-27

As the Holy Spirit controls the believer, He also empowers the believer to witness to others with power that others may drink of this living water for eternal life.

JUNE 14   DEUTERONOMY 18:15-22

Write the verse(s) from your bible here. Then
write how you think it touches you.

JUNE 15   PHILIPPIANS 2:12-18

Write the verse(s) from your bible here. Then
write how you think it touches you.

165

JUNE 16   ACTS 26:15-18

Write the verse(s) from your bible here. Then
write how you think it touches you.

JUNE 17 MATTHEW 13:54-58

Write the verse(s) from your bible here. Then
write how you think it touches you.

JUNE 18 ACTS 12:6-10

Write the verse(s) from your bible here. Then
write how you think it touches you.

JUNE 19   MATTHEW 13:10-17

Why Jesus Used Parables

Write the verse(s) from your bible here. Then
write how you think it touches you.

JUNE 20   JOHN 7:15-19

Write the verse(s) from your bible here. Then
write how you think it touches you.

JUNE 21　JOHN 15:18-25

Write the verse(s) from your bible here. Then
write how you think it touches you.

JUNE 22   JOHN 15:26-17

Write the verse(s) from your bible here. Then
write how you think it touches you.

JUNE 23   JOHN 15:9-17

Write the verse(s) from your bible here. Then
write how you think it touches you.

JUNE 24   JOHN 15:1-7

Write the verse(s) from your bible here. Then
write how you think it touches you.

JUNE 25 ECCLESIASTES 1:3-11

Write the verse(s) from your bible here. Then
write how you think it touches you.

The Emptiness of Pleasure

Write the verse(s) from your bible here. Then
write how you think it touches you.

JUNE 27   ECCLESIASTES 2:4-11

The Emptiness of Possessions

Write the verse(s) from your bible here. Then
write how you think it touches you.

———————————————————

JUNE 28   ECCLESIASTES 2:12-17

The Relative Value of Wisdom

Write the verse(s) from your bible here. Then
write how you think it touches you.

JUNE 29   MATTHEW 18:15-20

Write the verse(s) from your bible here. Then
write how you think it touches you.

JUNE 30   NUMBERS 6:24-26

The LORD bless you and protect you;
The LORD make His face shine on you, and be gracious to you;
The LORD look on you with favor, and give you peace.

JULY 1   PROVERBS 18:21

Life and death are in the power of the tongue,
and those who love it will eat its fruit.

Teach a youth about the way he should go;
even when he is old he will not depart from it.

JULY 3   MARK 9: 33-36

Write the verse(s) from your bible here. Then
write how you think it touches you.

JULY 4

The current version of the Pledge of Allegiance reads:

I pledge allegiance to the flag of the United States of America and to the republic for which it stands: one nation under God, indivisible, with liberty and justice for all.

JULY 5   MARK 12:13-17

God and Caesar

Write the verse(s) from your bible here. Then
write how you think it touches you.

JULY 6

What do you feel deep in your spirit that you want to do?
Make preparations to do…

Psalm 37:4

———————————————

God places (or gives) desire in our hearts…
He will help us fulfill them.

———————————————

JULY 7

The Lenten Pretzel

The pretzel is actually the Lenten bread of classical Christianity. In the 400's, because the fast was so strict (e.g. no eggs or butter), Roman Christians made bread during Lent out of flour, water, and salt. And to remind themselves that Lent was a time of prayer, they shaped the bread in the form of praying arms (before the gesture of folded hands, Christians used to pray with their arms crossed in front of them). They called these breads **bracellae**, Latin for "little arms," and from this term, our word "pretzel".

JULY 8

The 4 candles in an advent wreath stand for: _____

Preparation

_____   _____   _____

Hope   joy   love

Hope, Preparation, Joy, Love

This last candle we light for _____

Christ

What does this mean to me at Christmas time?

_____

JULY 9

The enemy is watching me; watching to find out my desire; to turn my desire in to desperation.

My value in God, as a child of God, is of immense value. God, fill me with you, allow me to focus on you and your word, then allow me to make decisions based on you.

JULY 10   PSALM 37:14-17

Write the verse(s) from your bible here. Then
write how you think it touches you.

For am I now trying to win the favor of people, or God?
Or am I striving to please people? If I were still trying
to please people, I would not be a slave of Christ.
If I want their approval, I am their slave...
(society, gangs, friends...)

JULY 12   RESPECT

Treating others the way you want to be treated.
Showing kindness and consideration;
Liking yourself enough to be yourself.
Accepting others for who they are.

JULY 13 JEREMIAH 29:11-14

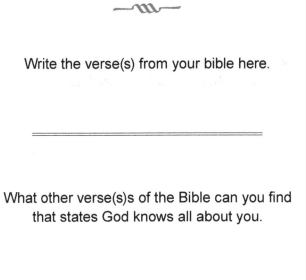

Write the verse(s) from your bible here.

—————————————————

What other verse(s)s of the Bible can you find
that states God knows all about you.

—————————————————

Write the verse(s) from your bible here. Then
write how you think it touches you.

JULY 15   JOEL 2:25-27

Write the verse(s) from your bible here. Then
write how you think it touches you.

════════════════════════════════

JULY 16   REVELATIONS 12:10-12

Write the verse(s) from your bible here. Then
write how you think it touches you.

JULY 17   HEBREWS 9:11-14

Write the verse(s) from your bible here. Then
write how you think it touches you.

JULY 18   CREED

I believe in God, the Father almighty,
Creator of heaven and earth.
I believe in Jesus Christ, his only son, our Lord.
He was conceived by the power of the Holy Spirit,
born of the Virgin Mary.
He suffered under Pontius Pilate, was
crucified, died, and was buried.
He descended into hell,
On the third day he rose again.
He ascended into heaven,
is seated at the right hand of the Father.
He will come again to judge the living and the dead.
I believe in the Holy Spirit
The holy catholic Church
The communion of saints
The forgiveness of sins
The resurrection of the body,
and life everlasting.
Amen

JULY 19

Create in me a clean hear O God,
renew a right spirit within me.
Cast me not away from your presence,
take not your Holy Spirit from me.
Restore to me the joy of your salvation,
uphold me with your free spirit.

JULY 20

The Ten Commandments Then God spoke all these words:

I am the LORD your God, who brought you out of the land of Egypt, out of the place of slavery. Do not have other gods besides Me.

Do not make an idol for yourself, whether in the shape of anything in the heavens above or on the earth below or in the waters under the earth. You must not bow down to them or worship them; for I, the LORD your God, am a jealous God, punishing the children for the fathers' sin, to the third and fourth generations of those who hate Me, but showing faithful love to a thousand generations of those who love Me and keep My commands.

Do not misuse the name of the LORD your God, because the LORD will punish anyone who misuses His name.

Remember to dedicate the Sabbath day: You are to labor six days and do all your work, but the seventh day is a Sabbath to the LORD your God. You must not do any work—you, your son or daughter, your male or female slave, your livestock, or the foreigner who is within your gates. For the LORD made the heavens and the earth, the sea, and everything in them in six days; then He rested on the seventh day. Therefore the LORD blessed the Sabbath day and declared it holy.

Honor your father and your mother so that you may have a long life in the land that the LORD your God is giving you.

Do not murder.

Do not commit adultery.

Do not steal.

Do not give false testimony against your neighbor.

Do not covet your neighbor's house. Do not covet your neighbor's wife, his male or female slave, his ox or donkey, or anything that belongs to your neighbor.

JULY 21   ROMANS 13:9-10

Write the verse(s) from your bible here. Then
write how you think it touches you.

JULY 22 EXODUS 24:3-12

Write the verse(s) from your bible here. Then
write how you think it touches you.

JULY 23   COLOSSIANS 3:12-17

The Christian Life

Write the verse(s) from your bible here. Then
write how you think it touches you.

_____

JULY 24   COLOSSIANS 3:18-25

Christ in Your Home

Write the verse(s) from your bible here. Then
write how you think it touches you.

JULY 25   1SAMUEL 2:18-26

Write the verse(s) from your bible here. Then
write how you think it touches you.

Creation's Praise of the LORD
Hallelujah!

Write the verse(s) from your bible here. Then
write how you think it touches you.

JULY 27   LUKE 2:41-50

In His Father's House

Write the verse(s) from your bible here. Then
write how you think it touches you.

JULY 28

Confession of Forgiveness

I confess that I am in bondage to sin and cannot free myself
I have sinned against you in thought, word, and deed
By what I have done and what I have left undone
I have not loved you with my whole heart;
I have not loved my neighbors as myself.
For the sake of you Son, Jesus Christ,
have mercy on me, forgive me, renew me,
and lead me so that I have delight in your will,
And walk in your ways,
To the glory of your holy name.
Amen

JULY 29   MICAH 5:2-6

Write the verse(s) from your bible here. Then
write how you think it touches you.

JULY 30   PSALM 80

Write the verse(s) from your bible here. Then
write how you think it touches you.

JULY 31   HEBREWS 10:5-10

—ɯ—

Write the verse(s) from your bible here. Then
write how you think it touches you.

AUGUST 1   1 TIMOTHY 4:6-10

A Good Servant of Jesus Christ

Write the verse(s) from your bible here. Then
write how you think it touches you.

AUGUST 2   1 TIMOTHY 4: 11-16

Instructions for Ministry

Write the verse(s) from your bible here. Then
write how you think it touches you.

AUGUST 3   JAMES 2:14-26

Faith and Works

Write the verse(s) from your bible here. Then write how you think it touches you.

AUGUST 4   JUDE 1:5-11

Write the verse(s) from your bible here. Then
write how you think it touches you.

AUGUST 5   ROMANS 12:1-2

A Living Sacrifice

Write the verse(s) from your bible here. Then
write how you think it touches you.

AUGUST 6　ROMANS 12:3-8

Many Gifts but One Body

Write the verse(s) from your bible here. Then
write how you think it touches you.

AUGUST 7 ROMANS 12:9-21

Christian Ethics

Write the verse(s) from your bible here. Then
write how you think it touches you.

<hr>═══════════════════════════════════</hr>

AUGUST 8   ROMANS 13:8-11

Love Our Primary Duty

Write the verse(s) from your bible here. Then
write how you think it touches you.

AUGUST 9   DEUTERONOMY 6:4-9

Write the verse(s) from your bible here. Then
write how you think it touches you.

AUGUST 10   DEUTERONOMY 11:13-25

Write the verse(s) from your bible here. Then
write how you think it touches you.

AUGUST 11 1 PETER 3:13-18

Write the verse(s) from your bible here. Then
write how you think it touches you.

AUGUST 12 ISAIAH 1:18-19

Write the verse(s) from your bible here. Then
write how you think it touches you.

AUGUST 13　HEBREWS 11:1-10

Write the verse(s) from your bible here. Then
write how you think it touches you.

AUGUST 14   2 PETER 1:19-21

Write the verse(s) from your bible here. Then
write how you think it touches you.

AUGUST 15 HEBREWS 12:14-23

Write the verse(s) from your bible here. Then
write how you think it touches you.

AUGUST 16   MATTHEW 1:18-25

The Nativity of the Messiah

Write the verse(s) from your bible here. Then
write how you think it touches you.

AUGUST 17

When you see the manger where Christ was born, do you also see the cross Christ died and was resurrected on?

AUGUST 18

In Genesis 1, write down all the characters of God that are given
to you. Your creator's character and why he created you.

AUGUST 19   1 CORINTHIANS 1:3-9

Grace to you and peace from God our
Father and the Lord Jesus Christ.

I always thank my God for you because of God's grace given
to you in Christ Jesus, that by Him you were made rich in
everything—in all speaking and all knowledge—as the testimony
about Christ was confirmed among you, so that you do not lack
any spiritual gift as you eagerly wait for the revelation of our Lord
Jesus Christ. He will also confirm you to the end, blameless
in the day of our Lord Jesus Christ. God is faithful; by Him you
were called into fellowship with His Son, Jesus Christ our Lord.

AUGUST 20   REVELATIONS 12:11-12

Write theverse(s) from your bible here. Then
write how you think it touches you.

AUGUST 21   REVELATIONS 20:1-3

Write the verse(s) from your bible here. Then
write how you think it touches you.

AUGUST 22 REVELATIONS 20:4-6

The Saints Reign with the Messiah

Write the verse(s) from your bible here. Then
write how you think it touches you.

_____

AUGUST 23   LEVITICUS 18:21-29

Write the verse(s) from your bible here. Then
write how you think it touches you.

AUGUST 24   LEVITICUS 23

Seven Yearly Festivals

Passover

Christ Crucified the evening before Passover
Reminded the Israelites of the deliverance from
Egypt when death passed over their homes.

Unleaven bread

Christ, the sinless sacrifice, was in the tomb
Reminded the Israelites of their quick departure
from Egypt (bread without leaven)

Firstfruits

Christ was alive and seen as the firstfruits of the
resurrection of the dead. To celebrate the first
visible ripening of the barley harvest.

Pentecost

The birth of the Christian church occurred in
Jerusalem on Pentecost. A reminder of God
reveling the Law to Moses on Mt Sinai.

Trumpets

Commemoration and jubilation— return of Christ
A memorial of blowing trumpets

Day of Atonement To make atonement for yourselves before the
LORD your God, picture of the coming judgments
of God, called the Tribulation. When the high
priest would atone for Israel's sins.

Tabernacles

A picture of the future reign of the Messiah in
Jerusalem. Remember the 40 years of Israel
wandering in the wilderness.

The Baptism of Our Lord cannot help but recall our own, and all baptismal blessings. We recall and celebrate our adoption as children of God, the gift of the Holy Spirit, and the promised company of almighty God when we "pass through the waters... the rivers... fire." On this day the heavens open again, for the assembly, and we receive the gift of the beloved Son of God in bread and wine.

Prayer

Almighty God, you anointed Jesus at His baptism with the Holy Spirit and revealed him as your beloved Son. Keep all who are born of water and the Spirit faithful in your service, that we may rejoice to be called Your children, children of God, through Jesus Christ, our Savior and Lord, who lives and reigns with you and the Holy Spirit, one God, now and forever.
In the name of your son Jesus Christ,
Amen

AUGUST 26

We as Christians received God's grace daily. Have you
ever taken advantage of God's grace? Cheap grace?
Be honest. Explain what is cheap grace and how can
we not fall into the trap of expecting cheap grace?

AUGUST 27

Heavenly father, in your grace and mercy on this day, I ask
that you forgive my sins, known and unknown. I ask for
release and give me direction to follow your every command.
Forgive my questions and allow answers as it is your will.

Those in my heart need:

I ask all this in the name of your son, Jesus Christ. Amen.

AUGUST 28

Close your eyes and imagine you are in the
judgment of God; what is your question?

AUGUST 29

Self-esteem is a fragile, and can be crushed so easily. Satan tries to destroy you and your will daily. Through bombardment of technology, TV, & general chaos. Only being in the word of God can make a difference; and your focus on the one true God, & His word. How are you going to keep focused?

AUGUST 30

We mutter & Sputter, we fume & we spurt,
We mumble & grumble, our feeling get hurt.
We can't understand things, our vision grows dim;
When all that we need is a moment with Him.
What have you learned to do now?

AUGUST 31

The cross is the answer to man's predicament.
What is your predicament that the cross is the
answer to? Do you believe it is the answer?

SEPTEMBER 1

Five Finger Prayer

Your thumb is nearest to you.
Begin you prayers by praying for those closest to you.
They are the easiest to remember
The next finger is the pointing finger.
Pray for those who teach, instruct, and heal.
This includes teachers, doctors, and ministers.
They need support and wisdom in pointing
others in the right direction.
Keep them in your prayers.
The next finger is the tallest finger.
It reminds us of our leaders.
Pray for the president, government leaders, and leaders
in business, industry & administrators. These people
shape our nations and guide public opinion.
They need God's guidance.
The forth finger is our ring finger.
Surprising to many is the fact that this is our weakest
finger; as any piano teacher will testify. It should
remind us to pray for those who are weak, in trouble,
or in pain. They need our prayers day and night.
You cannot pray to much for them.
Lastly comes our little finger; the smallest finger of all
This is where we should place ourselves
in relation to God and others.
As the bible says, "The least shall be the greatest among you,"
Your pinkie should remind you to pray for yourself.
By the time you have prayed for the other four groups,
your own needs will be put into proper perspective, &
you will be able to pray for yourself more effectively.
Author unknown

SEPTEMBER 2   ECCLESIASTES 2:18-26

The Emptiness of Work

Write the verse(s) from your bible here. Then
write how you think it touches you.

SEPTEMBER 3

Look up the word "forgiven" in a thesaurus. How many other words could describe how God forgives?

SEPTEMBER 4

Look up the word "surrender" in a dictionary, and
then in a thesaurus. Christ did this for you.

SEPTEMBER 5

As you read the book of Ester, could you step out
in faith and trust God in all obedience?

Take into account she was alone in her faith. She
lost her parents, was taken for her land and her
comforts. The only trust worthy person she had was
outside of her walls... through secret messages.

SEPTEMBER 6

As you read the book of Ruth, think of how you would deal with the situation in the less judgment of today's world. Would you take care of your mother-in-law if her husband pasted on?

Would you continue to care for her after your husband past on? Keep in mind at this point in Ruth's life she had little to no contact with her family, and there were no children involved; And one daughter-in-law did go back to her family.

SEPTEMBER 7

Do you fight to keep your life simple, uncomplicated,
and ruled only by the word of God?

At Christmas do you have to buy all a gift, or is the
fellowship of loved ones enough for you?

SEPTEMBER 8   ZECHARIAH 8:16-17

Write the verse(s) from your bible here. Then
write how you think it touches you.

SEPTEMBER 9   ZEPHANIAH 4:3-17

He laughs, He feels for me…

Write the verse(s) from your bible here. Then
write how you think it touches you.

Jesus Wept.

Jesus had a friend; the friend was sick and died. Even knowing what He could do, Jesus had compassion for His friend. The Lord, Jesus Christ, felt as you and I feel, do you comprehend that Christ FEELS for you also?

SEPTEMBER 11

God is in control of all; the earthquakes, the rain, mudslides,
and the events of each day. Are we so spoiled to think
by living in the borders of the United States no one can
hurt or attack us? We were taught otherwise.
When the London subway was bombed did you feel as horrified?
When an Italian hotel was bombed, did you feel as horrified?

SEPTEMBER 12

Everything you have belongs to God. He has given it to you to distribute as a good steward. How are you going to do this? Tithe to the church of money and time?

SEPTEMBER 13

Are you familiar with your health? Are you aware of what food is good and what food is not good for your health? Do you have health problems that food would help correct?

SEPTEMBER 14

Do you eat to live or live to eat? It makes a difference to how you live. Does God care how you eat? The body holds the Holy Spirit if you are a believer, which makes it God's temple...YES he cares!

SEPTEMBER 15

Do you pray before each meal and ask God to Bless the food for the nourishment of the body and for the good of His Kingdom...

SEPTEMBER 16

Do you believe that the mind, body, and spirit are one? and if one is ill, all suffer? How could you balance your life to include all?

SEPTEMBER 17

How is Satan putting fear into your life? Conquer it by
praying and replacing fear with courage. (See Judges 6)

False
Evidence
Appearing
Real

SEPTEMBER 18

Do you hold yourself accountable for your actions? The
same way you hold others accountable for theirs?
Begin today to live according to the commandments.
Begin to understand how simple it can be, how attainable it is.

SEPTEMBER 19

What is the difference between need and want? What does God give me? How is that not enough?

SEPTEMBER 20

What is the difference between sufficient and satisfactory?
Look up in the dictionary and thesaurus.

SEPTEMBER 21   PSALM 46:10

What does it mean to you to be still?

Write the verse(s) from your bible here. Then
write how you think it touches you.

SEPTEMBER 22   MATTHEW 14:22-32

God stays the same; we must change to be more like
Him. Learn to change with God, as His servant.

Write the verse(s) from your bible here. Then
write how you think it touches you.

SEPTEMBER 23   MATTHEW 24:36-44

No one knows how or when the second coming
of Christ will be, "only the father knows".
Just as we prepare daily for our schedules of life, adapting to
the unexpected, and the expected for the coming day; we must
also prepare our spirit and our mind for the day of His glory.

Write the verse(s) from your bible here. Then
write how you think it touches you.

SEPTEMBER 24 MATTHEW 24:45-51

Do unto others...one day the tables will turn and you
will be the one being in the judgment seat.

Write the verse(s) from your bible here. Then
write how you think it touches you.

SEPTEMBER 25   HEBREW 12:6-8

Write the verse(s) from your bible here. Then
write how you think it touches you.

SEPTEMBER 26   HEBREWS 13:8-9

We change to be more like Him. We evolve
to more loving and Christ like.

Write the verse(s) from your bible here. Then
write how you think it touches you.

===

With all the action, noise, and chaos vying for your attention, how do you hear Him? Satan likes it this way; creating distractions and taking the attention away from what you want to do. Take control and look to God.

Write the verse(s) from your bible here. Then write how you think it touches you.

_____

SEPTEMBER 28   2 SAMUEL 10:1-19

Have you ever tried to help, assist, or care for someone
and the actions were taken the opposite as it was
intended? And then turned into a big problem?

Write the verse(s) from your bible here. Then
write how you think it touches you.

In the true light there is only the fact that
God knows what is in your heart.

Write the verse(s) from your bible here. Then
write how you think it touches you.

Write the verse(s) from your bible here. Then
write how you think it touches you.

Each day we awaken, is a new beginning of today to
correct the faults of yesterday. Take the opportunity
now. Tomorrow is a guarantee to come.

Write the verse(s) from your bible here. Then
write how you think it touches you.

———————————————————

Worry is not part of God's plan. He is in control,
and faith in Him eliminates worry. Release control
to Him and His blessings will abound.

———————————————————

OCTOBER 2   1 CORINTHIANS 12:4-11

Write the verse(s) from your bible here. Then
write how you think it touches you.

OCTOBER 3   PHILIPPIANS 4:19

Write the verse(s) from your bible here. Then
write how you think it touches you.

———————————————————

God knows our needs before we do, and
supplies each at the exact perfect time.

———————————————————

OCTOBER 4　MATTHEW 8:28-29

Write the verse(s) from your bible here. Then
write how you think it touches you.

===

If you ever wondered if there were demons or not...

They are real, they called Him my name, and
they know of the time they have left.

===

OCTOBER 5   ACTS 2:22-24

Write the verse(s) from your bible here. Then
write how you think it touches you.

_____

He is for real; from God.

_____

OCTOBER 6   1 CORINTHIANS 1: 17-18

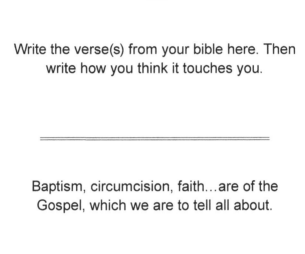

Write the verse(s) from your bible here. Then
write how you think it touches you.

=================================

Baptism, circumcision, faith...are of the
Gospel, which we are to tell all about.

=================================

OCTOBER 7   GALATIANS 2:20

Write the verse(s) from your bible here. Then
write how you think it touches you.

OCTOBER 8   GALATIANS 6:14

Write the verse(s) from your bible here. Then
write how you think it touches you.

Angels are messengers for God. They are not human, cannot become human, cannot reproduce. God created as His servant's.

Can you compare and contrast worshipping
God & worshipping idols:

Worship God   **Worship Idols**

Unseen worship   Visible worship

My action is the only visibility of my faith All
can see what I am and what I have

OCTOBER 11   JUDGES CHAPTER 4

What do you think of Deborah being a prophetess, a judge of Israel?

God's ways are not our ways? Do we need to adjust to God's ways?

OCTOBER 12   ISAIAH 12:2-6

Write the verse(s) from your bible here. Then
write how you think it touches you.

OCTOBER 13

Read Judges Chapter 5

A victory over war (from the reading in Judges
Chapter 4). Victory song after a

war, joyous celebration for God's victory.

What adjustments are necessary for you to
see this as the "Glory to God"?

OCTOBER 14

Will it help if we look at who Deborah was?

Deborah was the Fourth Judge of Israel, but the only female judge
God gave her special gifts to talk to people,
advise & counsel those around her
When Deborah was to lead, she was wise
to plan, direct, and delegate

God chooses leaders by his standards alone
Leaders should pray for which people will be good helpers

Deborah was Prophetess and Judge in Canaan
Deborah's husband, Lapidoth

OCTOBER 15

We all have read Genesis 2 several times, almost to the point we could recite the facts without reading it. But this time, read Genesis 2 with concentration on Eve and the Creator: Who, what, where, when, why, and how?

OCTOBER 16

Look the word "Grace" up in the dictionary. Write it below.

Write what you believe grace is.

Now define what God's grace is.

OCTOBER 17   GENESIS 15

Sarah, wife of Abraham. There probably is not another wife
with the patience of Sarah or the obedience of Sarah.
Would you immediately start packing when your spouse
came home and said someone told him to move, so
were moving...Tents, animals, servants and all.
On way we wait, short or long wait, is we devise our own plan
and "help" God with our agenda... Not knowing the power
of the almighty God, she suggested Hagar as the surrogate
for her child. It was not God's plan though. What could have
both of them have done before taking their own action?

OCTOBER 18

Who was *Sarah* ?

We see Sarah as a strong example of a woman
Sarah was extremely loyal to her son
Sarah was the mother of a nation that was promised to Abraham
Sarah would be our ancestor and is in the linage of Jesus
She was a strong woman of faith
In Hebrews 11 Sarah is the first woman listed in the Hall of Faith

Sarah shows us its normal but foolish to have
trouble believing God's promises
As we attempt to work out problems, go to God for consul first
We learn to be accountable for our actions and not blame others

God responds to our walk of faith, even
when we feel we have failed
God is not bound by what logically could happen; he
stretches the limits and causes unusual events to occur

Do you see yourself in any part of Sarah?

OCTOBER 19

Hagar was the Mother of Abraham's first child, Ishmael
Ishmael is founder of the Arab Nations

When Hagar was faced with challenges, she tended to turn away
Hagar's son brought out strong feelings
of pride and arrogance in her

God is always faithful in his plans and promises
When we complicate the process with our
own agenda, His plan prevails
God knows us & wants to have a relationship with each of us
Do you know a person like Hagar who would pursue
favor with God by their own agenda, instead of
trusting in His mercy and forgiveness?

Any part of you in this?

OCTOBER 20

When Rebekah was confronted with a need, she
immediately acted without thinking it through
She could only see what she wanted in the end

Her decisions were not always balanced by wisdom
Rebekah had a favorite child, which always hurts a family
Rebekah seemed to always try trickery on her husband

If our actions are not guided by God, they are not justified
God uses each of His children in his plan... even
through our bad decisions and miss-judgments

Do you see any part of yourself in her?

OCTOBER 21

Rachel was loyal to her family
Rachel was the mother of Joseph & Benjamin

Rachel's envy & competitiveness destroyed
her relationship with sister, Leah.
Rachel took her loyalty to far and was capable of dishonesty
Jacob was never able to convince Rachel that his devotion
did not depend on her ability to have children

Loyalty should be controlled by what is true and right
Love is freely given and accepted, not earned

Do you see any part of yourself in her?

Miriam was a quick thinker under pressure, an
able leader, songwriter and prophetess

Miriam was jealous of Moses' authority, and was disciplined
for it when she openly criticized Moses' leadership

We see through Miriam that there may be motives behind criticism,
& often more important to deal with the motives than the criticism

Do you see any part of yourself in her?

OCTOBER 23

Rahab was a relative of Boaz, an ancestor
of David & in the linage of Jesus
One of only two women listed in the Hall of Faith in Hebrews 11
Resourceful, willing to help others at great cost to herself

Even though she was a prostitute, she did not allow
that mistake in life to define her forever.

She did not let fear overcome her faith in
God's ability to deliver His promises

Do you see any part of yourself in her?

OCTOBER 24

Deliah was persistent when faced with challenges

Deliah valued money more than people…it was her idol
She betrayed the man who trusted her

We see from her example that we need to choose carefully
when we place our trust in people. Trust is earned and shared

Do you see any part of yourself in her?

OCTOBER 25

We see through Ruth & Naomi that a relationship's
greatest bond is faith in God
Each person must have a relationship with God,
& must have a strong mutual commitment
Ruth & Naomi tried to do what was best for
the other, compassion and unselfish

We see through each of them that God's presence
in a relationship will overcome differences that
otherwise create division and distrust

Do you see any part of yourself in them?

OCTOBER 26

Hannah was the mother of Samuel, Israel's greatest judge
She was fervent in worship, passionate in prayer, &
willing to follow through on a costly commitment.

Hannah, like many of us, struggled with her sense of self-
worth because of something she determined, not God

Through Hannah we see that God hears & answers prayer
We see our children are gifts from God, & God is
concerned for the oppressed and afflicted

Do you see any part of yourself in her?

OCTOBER 27

Abigail was considered sensible and capable
She was a persuasive speaker, able to see the overall picture

Abigail's life's is an example of how tough
situations bring out the best in people
She also did not need a prestigious title
to play a significant role in life

Do you see any part of yourself in her? 1 Samuel 25-2 Samuel 2.

Michal loved David & was his first wife; She saved
David's life & thought and acted quickly

Michal had a bad habit of lying under pressure; She allowed
herself to become resentful over some of her circumstances. In
her unhappiness, she was jealous over David's love for God

Michal is an example of how we may not responsible
for what happens to us, but we are responsible for how
we respond to our circumstances. Disobedience to
God always has consequences to us, & could harm others

Do you see any part of yourself in her?

Bathsheba became influential in the kingdom
of David, alongside her son Solomon; Israel's
wisest king & an ancestor of Jesus Christ.

Bathsheba willingly committed Adultery; we may feel
caught up in a chain of events, but we are still responsible
for our actions & how we participate in those events

Bathsheba shows us a sin may begin like a small seed, but the
harvest of consequences could be beyond your comprehension

Do you see any part of yourself in her?

Jezebel eliminated disciples of God in Israel. She
promoted, funded & supported Baal worship.

She threatened to kill Elijah; she believed kings and queens
could do or have anything, & used these strong convictions to
do or get whatever she needed to accomplish her agenda.

Jezebel is an example showing us that committed
and sincere is not always enough.

Jezebel is proof that rejecting God always leads to disaster

Do you see any part of yourself in her?

OCTOBER 31 PSALM 37:8-13

Write the verse(s) from your bible here. Then
write how you think it touches you.

NOVEMBER 1

All saints day

What is a Saint? Why a Saint? Do you
think you have saints in your life?

How would a Godly mentor help you in your life?
Shouldn't everyone have a mentor? Accountable to &
responsible for? Should you also be a mentor?

Be very careful. There is a fine line between a mentor and an idol. God commands us not to have idols. How would you guard against idols? We are all to have Godly mentors; We are all to go to members in the body of Christ for assistance and help.

If it helps to define each one, think of the difference between someone who assists you and someone you "idolize" and follow blindly.

NOVEMBER 4

We have looked at several people in the bible (October).
Do you believe they are your ancestors?

Why or why not?

_____

NOVEMBER 5

Do you believe the bible is real and an instruction book for life?

Why do you feel this way?

NOVEMBER 6   PSALM 42

Write the verse(s) from your bible here. Then
write how you think it touches you.

NOVEMBER 7

Thoughts and response to Psalm 42

There may come times when after thirsting for God, weeping for his help, and enduring ridicule, we still do not hear his voice. Such times often lead to depression and discouragement, but the psalmist discovered a remedy. He remembered God's great blessing; he realized that although God seemed silent, he was with him: he gazed upon God's beautiful creation that proclaims his love. The psalmist had felt billows of sorrow, but he realized that he was never adrift from God's steadfast love. Finally he faithfully expected God to act. When you cannot seem to find God use this remedy and you will once again find reason to praise him.

Her attractiveness comes entirely from her character.

The woman described in this chapter has outstanding abilities. Her family's social position is high. It may not be one woman, but a composite portrait of ideal woman-hood. Do not see her as a model or imitate every detail; your days are not long enough to do all. See her instead as an inspiration to be all you can be. We can't be just like her, but we can learn from her integrity and resourcefulness.

NOVEMBER 9

Name the 12 disciples, and there Occupation

NOVEMBER 10

Salvation's Freeway

Romans 3:23   All but one has sinned
Romans 6:23   The penalty for our sin is death
Romans 5:8   Jesus Christ died for sin
Romans 10:8-10   To be forgiven for our sin, we
must believe and confess that Jesus is LORD.
Salvation domes through Jesus Christ.

God's sovereignty; Most of the world is worshiping the beast, the Antichrist, whom they believe has all power and authority.

His entrance signals the end of false powers.

The battle lines have been drawn.

What is your feeling?

When Moses led the Israelites out of Egypt,
which way did God direct them?
Which way was the Promised Land?

In Psalm 46:10 God tells us to be still and know He is God.
Yet Satan says go, do something, make a name for yourself.

Why do you think God's way is so different,
yet we want to believe Satan's lies?

NOVEMBER 14

Go to the map in your bible; How many
tribes were given lots of land?

What tribe did Jesus Christ come through?

---

12 Judah

NOVEMBER 15

Who was Saul of Tarsus and what is his apostle's name?

Paul   Timothy

My life is never left to chance; I am not a slave of fate;
luck is not a part of it; all of life has a purpose.

NOVEMBER 17

The enemy cannot hear what's in your head, but he's forced to hear what comes out of your mouth.

Give all to God so he has total control of all your fears. "Your word resonates in my spirit."

NOVEMBER 18   MICAH 7:8-10, 18-20

Write the verse(s) from your bible here. Then
write how you think it touches you.

NOVEMBER 19   1 PETER 1:3-6

Write the verse(s) from your bible here. Then
write how you think it touches you.

NOVEMBER 20   READ ACTS 2

Outpouring of the Holy Spirit   Then write
how you think it touches you.

NOVEMBER 21   EPHESIANS 1:13-14

Write the verse(s) from your bible here. Then
write how you think it touches you.

NOVEMBER 22   READ REVELATION 21:1-7

Write the verse(s) from your bible here. Then
write how you think it touches you.

NOVEMBER 23   MATTHEW 6:14-15

Write the verse(s) from your bible here. Then
write how you think it touches you.

Thanksgiving

Write the verse(s) from your bible here. Then
write how you think it touches you.

We always thank God, the Father of our Lord Jesus Christ, when
we pray for you, for we have heard of your faith in Christ Jesus
and of the love you have for all the saints because of the hope
reserved for you in heaven. You have already heard about [this
hope] in the message of truth, the gospel that has come to you.
It is bearing fruit and growing all over the world, just as it has
among you since the day you heard it and recognized God's
grace in the truth. You learned this from Epaphras, our much
loved fellow slave. He is a faithful minister of the Messiah on
your behalf, and he has told us about your love in the Spirit.

NOVEMBER 25   READ COLOSSIANS 2:13-15

Write the verse(s) from your bible here. Then
write how you think it touches you.

Thanksgiving

Write the verse(s) from your bible here. Then
write how you think it touches you.

———————————————————

I always thank my God for you because of God's grace given
to you in Christ Jesus, that by Him you were made rich in
everything—in all speaking and all knowledge—as the testimony
about Christ was confirmed among you, so that you do not lack
any spiritual gift as you eagerly wait for the revelation of our Lord
Jesus Christ. He will also confirm you to the end, blameless
in the day of our Lord Jesus Christ. God is faithful; by Him you
were called into fellowship with His Son, Jesus Christ our Lord.

———————————————————

NOVEMBER 27   READ COLOSSIANS 2:11-23

Write the verse(s) from your bible here. Then
write how you think it touches you.

NOVEMBER 28   1 THESSALONIANS 5:9-11

Write the verse(s) from your bible here. Then
write how you think it touches you.

The events of Christ's return

Christ will return visibly, with a loud command
There will be an unmistakable cry from an angel
There will be a trumpet fanfare such as has never been heard
Believers in Christ who are dead will rise from their graves
Believers who are alive will be caught up
in the clouds to meet Christ

While we may disagree about what events will lead up to
the return of Christ, there has been less disagreement
about what will happen once Christ does return.

Checklist for encouragers

Write the verse(s) from your bible here. Then
write how you think it touches you.

DECEMBER 1

Treatment of Church members 1 Timothy 5:1-16

Write the verse(s) from your bible here. Then
write how you think it touches you.

DECEMBER 2   ERROR & GREED   1 TIMOTHY 6:3-10

Write the verse(s) from your bible here. Then
write how you think it touches you.

DECEMBER 3

Leadership in the church Titus 1:1-16

Write the verse(s) from your bible here. Then
write how you think it touches you.

DECEMBER 4

Right living in the church Titus 2:1-15

Write the verse(s) from your bible here. Then
write how you think it touches you.

DECEMBER 5

Right living in society Titus 3:1-14

Write the verse(s) from your bible here. Then
write how you think it touches you.

DECEMBER 6

The new covenant is greater than the old Hebrews 8:1-8
Also see Psalm 110:4

Write the verse(s) from your bible here. Then
write how you think it touches you.

DECEMBER 7

The superiority of Faith Hebrews 10:19 – 13:12

Write the verse(s) from your bible here. Then
write how you think it touches you.

DECEMBER 8

Faith Hebrews Chapter 11

Write the verse(s) from your bible here. Then
write how you think it touches you.

DECEMBER 9

Moral Direction Hebrew Chapter 13

Write the verse(s) from your bible here. Then
write how you think it touches you.

DECEMBER 10   READ ISAIAH 63

Who is the enemy and who is the foe? Careful, careful...

DECEMBER 11   READ ISAIAH 56

Write the verse(s) from your bible here. Then
write how you think it touches you.

‗‗‗‗‗‗‗‗‗‗‗‗‗‗‗‗‗‗‗‗‗‗‗‗‗‗‗‗‗‗

Who are the gentiles? Are you a gentile?

‗‗‗‗‗‗‗‗‗‗‗‗‗‗‗‗‗‗‗‗‗‗‗‗‗‗‗‗‗‗

DECEMBER 12   READ ISAIAH 60

Patience & God's timing are not easy, but we must
remember God is in control of history… Time is only
of human flesh, God does not go by time.

DECEMBER 13   READ ISAIAH 49

Who is this Messiah that Isaiah prophecies?
How many years prior did he prophecy?

_____

DECEMBER 14   READ ISAIAH 53

Who is this humble and suffering servant?

_____

DECEMBER 15

Write the story of the birth of Christ as you know it. Don't look or review, just write it down. Then compare what you wrote with the story in Luke.

DECEMBER 16

Read John Chapter 1

What did you learn, recognize, forget and
reading made you remember.

DECEMBER 17

Read Luke Chapter 1

What did you learn, recognize, forget and
reading made you remember.

DECEMBER 18

What does the church mean to you? What is the church made up of; people or brick and mortar (the building). What is the church in the bible...
Read Acts 1.

DECEMBER 19

Read Matthew Chapter 1

When reading the first part, genealogy of 14 generations of Christ, think of your own family. Can you begin with yourself, and go back (5) five generations, then go back another (5), and another?

DECEMBER 20   ISAIAH 43:18-19

Write the verse(s) from your bible here. Then
write how you think it touches you.

_____

DECEMBER 21   ISAIAH 9:6-7

Write the verse(s) from your bible here. Then
write how you think it touches you.

DECEMBER 22 LUKE 2:8-20

The Shepherds and the Angels

Write the verse(s) from your bible here. Then write how you think it touches you.

===============================

DECEMBER 23

The "Western way" recognizes our birthday as the day we came into the world. Back in Jesus' time the birthday was the day of conception.
Go back 9 months from the day you were born, what is your birth date.

DECEMBER 24 REVELATION 1:3

Blessed is the one who reads, hears, obeys…

One day God's anger towards sin will be fully & completely
unleashed. Satan's defeat & punishment will be seen, along with
all of his agents. False religions will be judged & destroyed; God
will reward His faithful with eternal life, but those who choose
to refuse to believe in him will face eternal punishment.

DECEMBER 25

You are cordially invited to
A Birthday Celebration!!

Guest of Honor: Jesus Christ
Date: Everyday, Traditionally, December 25
But He's always around, so the date is flexible...
Time: Whenever you're ready.
(Please don't be late, or you will miss out on all the fun!)
Place: In your heart...He'll meet you there. (You'll hear Him knock.)
Attire: Come as you are... grubbies are okay.
He'll be washing your clothes anyway. He said something about
new white robes and crowns for everyone who stays till the last.
Tickets: Admission is free. He's already paid for everyone...
(He says you wouldn't have been able to afford it anyway...)
It cost Him everything He had. But you
do need to accept the ticket!!
Refreshments: New wine, bread and a far-
out drink He calls "Living Water."
Followed by a supper that promises to be out of this World!
Gift Suggestions: Your life. He's one of those people
who already has everything else. (He's very generous in
return; just wait until you see what He has for you)!
Entertainment:: Joy, Peace, Truth, light, Life, Love, Real
Happiness, Communion with God, Forgiveness, Miracles, Healing,
Power, Eternity in Paradise, Contentment, and much more!
(All "G" rated, so bring your family and friends).
R.S.V.P.! Very Important! He must know ahead so He can
reserve a spot for you at His table. Also, He's keeping a list of His
friends for future reference. He calls it the "Lamb's book of life".
Party being given by His Children (That's us!) Hope
to see you there! For those of you whom I will see
at the party, share this with someone today.

DECEMBER 26 ECCLESIASTES 3:16-22

The Mystery of Injustice and Death

Write the verse(s) from your bible here. Then
write how you think it touches you.

DECEMBER 27

Repentance is not regret. True repentance
always has humility associated to it.
Luke 15:17-20
Then we must claim it and move on. 2
Chron 6:37-38 and 2 Cor 7:10

We will always have the ones who disapprove, and
/ or despise our restoration. This could be from
within the family or from enemy forces.
Isaiah 54:15-17 If you are true, God does what He promises.

Write the verse(s) from your bible here. Then
write how you think it touches you.

The parable of the Wise and Foolish Virgins

Are you prepared and ready for Christ to come for the final time?

DECEMBER 30   ECCLESIASTES 3:9-15

What does the worker gain from his struggles?

Write the verse(s) from your bible here. Then
write how you think it touches you.

_____

DECEMBER 31   ECCLESIASTES 3:1-8

There is an occasion for everything,
and a time for every activity under heaven:

Write the verse(s) from your bible here. Then
write how you think it touches you.

<hr/>

REFERENCES

1. H.R.H. Wilhelmina, Lonely But Not Alone (New York; McGraw-Hill, 1959) From Corrie ten Boom – Her life Her Faith – A Biography by Carole C Carolson (Fleming H Revell Company, Old Tappan, NJ 1983)
2. Corrie ten Boom – Her life Her Faith – A Biography by Carole C Carolson (Fleming H Revell Company, Old Tappan, NJ 1983) PG 155
3. July 4; Pledge of Allegiance
   http://en.wikipedia.org/wiki/Pledge_of_allegience

Printed in the United States
By Bookmasters